This book is
presented to

David Hunnycutt

On the
occasion of
4-5-04

Copyright © 2000
by Jane Gibson

Printed in China

ISBN: 0-8054-3533-6

Published by
Broadman & Holman Publishers
Nashville, Tennessee 37234

All rights reserved. No portion of this publication
may be reproduced, stored in a retrieval system or
transmitted in any form by any means – electronic,
mechanical, photocopying, recording,
or any other – except for brief quotations
in printed reviews, without the prior
written permission of the publisher.

Teacher
Here's My Heart

By Jane Gibson

Teacher here's
my heart.
She may be just
a child to you.
But in this child
are all my
prayers and all
my dreams
come true.

*In her hand
I put this
apple, hoping
you will see,
not just a gift,
but more,
much more,
a message here
from me:*

*Teacher here's
my heart
for you to hold
and mold
and make.*

Just because it
always does,
a heart is
bound to break...
But I know
you will
understand, and
wipe away
the tears.

How do I know?
Because you're a
Teacher;
There's no greater
calling.
Prayers all around
you, like a gentle
rain, are falling.

Know that there are angels at your desk, at every chair, blessings in each book and heaven's helpers everywhere.

I know that you will hold his hand, and calm his little fears.

*May it remind
you of the heart
you kept a time
for me.*

And when you see an apple, wherever it might be,

Many times
I bless you,
Teacher,
all throughout
the day.
In my head
I hear the sweet
and gentle
words you'll say.

He will learn, not just to read and write and count from you; But more, he'll see the things that loving, patient teachers do...

And someday soon, all on her own, my child will come and say, "Teacher here's my heart", and you'll remember this first day.